It's My Body

Head

Lola Schaefer

www.raintreepublishers.co.uk
Visit our website to find out more information about **Raintree** books.

To order:
☎ Phone 44 (0) 1865 888112
🖹 Send a fax to 44 (0) 1865 314091
🖥 Visit the Raintree Bookshop at **www.raintreepublishers.co.uk** to browse our catalogue and order online.

First published in Great Britain by Raintree, Halley Court, Jordan Hill, Oxford OX2 8EJ, part of Harcourt Education.
Raintree is a registered trademark of Harcourt Education Ltd.

© Harcourt Education Ltd 2003
First published in paperback in 2004
The moral right of the proprietor has been asserted.

Editorial: Jennifer Gillis and Diyan Leake
Design: Sue Emerson (HL-US) and Michelle Lisseter
Picture Research: Jennifer Gillis
Production: Lorraine Hicks

Originated by Dot Gradations
Printed and bound in China by South China Printing Company

ISBN 1 844 21649 7 (hardback)
07 06 05 04 03
10 9 8 7 6 5 4 3 2 1

ISBN 1 844 21655 1 (paperback)
08 07 06 05 04
10 9 8 7 6 5 4 3 2 1

British Library Cataloguing in Publication Data
Schaefer, Lola
Head
612.9'1
A full catalogue record for this book is available from the British Library.

Acknowledgements
The publishers would like to thank the following for permission to reproduce photographs: Ann Purcell p. **17R**; Corbis pp. **5** (Annie Griffiths Belt), **12** (George Disario), **13** (LWA-Dann Tardif), **15** (Lindsay Hebberd); Custom Medical Stock Photo p. **23** (bone, brain, joint, muscle, skull); Heinemann Library pp. **6** (Brian Warling), **7** (Robert Lifson), **8** (Brian Warling), **9** (Brian Warling), **14** (Brian Warling), **16** (Brian Warling), **18** (Brian Warling), **19** (Brian Warling), **20** (Brian Warling), **21** (Brian Warling), **22** (Brian Warling), **23** (chin, forehead, Brian Warling), **24** (Brian Warling), back cover (neck, Robert Lifson; mouth, Brian Warling); PhotoEdit p. **4** (Richard Hutchings); PhotoTake p. **10** (BSIP); PictureQuest pp. **17R** (Carl Purcell/Words & Pictures), **17L** (Sue Klemens/Stock Boston, Inc.).

Cover photograph reproduced with permission of Zefa.

Every effort has been made to contact copyright holders of any material reproduced in this book. Any omissions will be rectified in subsequent printings if notice is given to the publishers.

Some words are shown in bold, **like this**. You can find them in the picture glossary on page 23.

Contents

What is my head?

Your head is part of your body.

Your body is made up of
many parts.

Each part of your body does a job.

You use different parts of your head
to think, talk, smell, see and hear.

Where is my head?

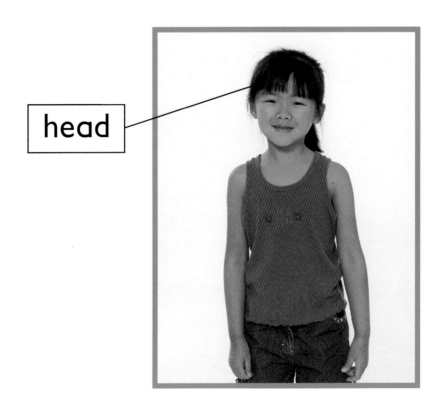

head

Your head is on top of your body.

Your neck joins your head to your body.

neck

You can move your head up
and down.

You can move it from side to side.

What are heads like?

There is hair on top of most heads.

Heads come in different shapes and sizes.

Grown-ups have bigger heads.

Children have smaller heads.

What is inside my head?

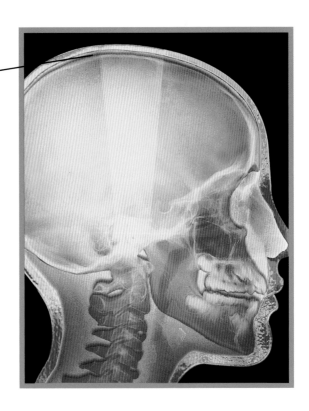

skull

There are **bones** inside your head.

Your **skull** is the bone that gives your head its shape.

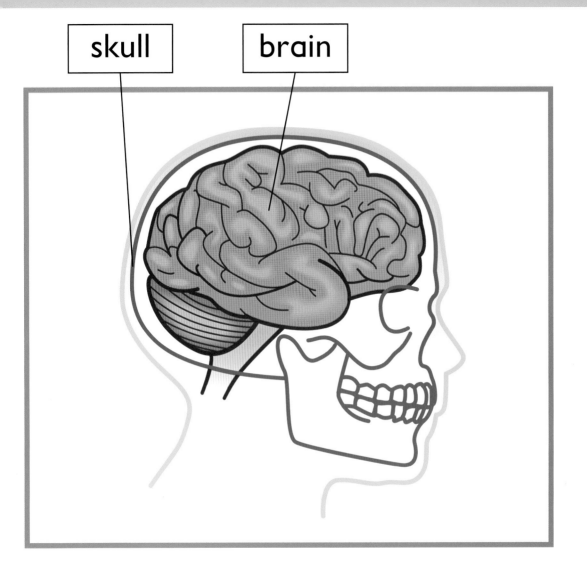

skull

brain

Your **brain** is inside your head.

Your skull keeps your brain safe.

What can I do with my head?

You use your eyes to see.

You use your mouth to talk, eat and breathe.

You use your ears to hear.

You use your nose to breathe and smell.

What is my face?

forehead

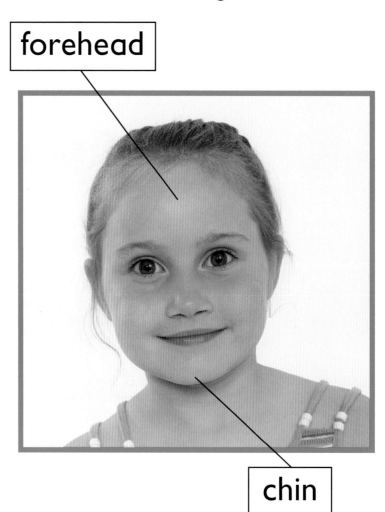

chin

Your face is the front part of your head.

The top part of your face is your **forehead**.

Your **chin** is at the bottom of your face.

Your mouth, nose and eyes are all parts of your face.

What do faces look like?

Faces can be full and round.

They can be long and thin.

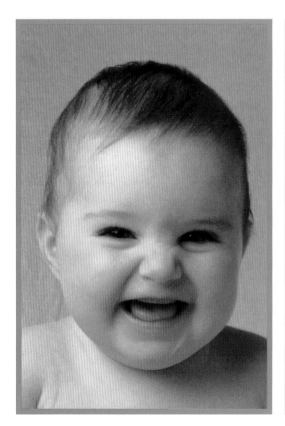 

Some faces have smooth skin.

Other faces have lots of wrinkles.

What is inside my face?

There are **bones** and **muscles** inside your face.

You use your muscles to move the parts of your face.

18

Your lips are the part of your mouth that you can see on your face.

When you open your mouth, you can see your teeth and tongue inside.

What can I do with my face?

Your face helps you show how you feel.

You can frown or cry.

You can make a funny face.

You can smile and laugh.

Quiz

Do you know what these are?

Look for the answers on page 24.

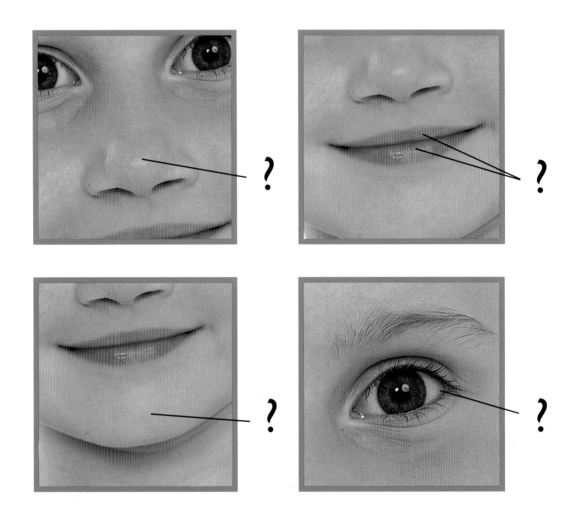

Glossary

bone
hard part inside your body

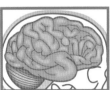

brain
the part of your body that controls all the other parts and which you think with

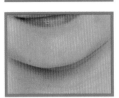

chin
the part at the bottom of your face

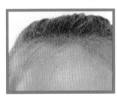

forehead
top part of the face

joint
a part of your body where bones come together so they can move

muscle
a part in your body that you use to move with

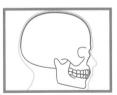

skull
the bony part of your head

Index

Answers to quiz on page 22

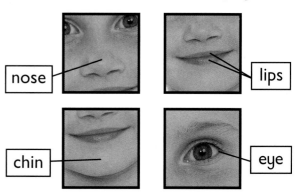

nose

lips

chin

eye